Puttenham People

Tales from a Surrey village

FOR
ESTHER

One faint line of manuscript in these oft mouldering documents is usually the only record of a long life of hardship and affliction as bravely and nobly borne as the difficulties, exploits and suffering of heroes perpetuated on the brass and marble of our stately cathedrals.

Charles Kerry, curate of Puttenham 1868-77,
writing about parish registers

Puttenham People

Tales from a Surrey village

Jock Vevers

Illustrations
Charles Bone PPRI ARCA

PUBLISHED BY SCREENTYPE 1991

Published by
Screentype Ltd
444 Brixton Road
London SW9

First published 1991

ISBN 0 9518044 0 5

Set in 11pt Caslon
by Screentype Ltd

Printed by
Headley Brothers Ltd
The Invicta Press
Queens Road
Ashford
Kent

Preface

These stories are based on events that have taken place in and around Puttenham in Surrey. They are true in their essentials and most of the characters are real people. Only two people have had other than their real names given to them. It's a very parochial book and it's about real local people and I apologize to anyone in the stories who does not like being in them and, of course, to the numerous others who are not mentioned. I'm afraid that as in most historical records the majority of the people are dead – that is not my fault. There are enough living to make it, I hope, of interest to the present inhabitants of this small Surrey village.

The book originates from stories told in Puttenham Church during the evenings of 'Words and Music' inspired by Paddy Smith and latterly, Stephen Wright, the organist. There is one story, however, which has rather less to do with the village and has a more general interest. I have put this at the end. Before those not interested in the concerns of this place turn to this story please promise to read it properly; I mean start at the beginning and read to the end. No peeking...

Any proceeds from this book beyond the costs are to be given by Charles Bone and myself for the benefit of Puttenham (Church of England) First School by kind permission of Celia Forbes, the headmistress.

Many thanks to Simon and Penny Vevers for their valuable help and to Jean Kerrigan for the design of the book.

R. G. (JOCK) VEVERS

Contents

The Australian and the ginger beer bottles

The Australian and the ginger beer bottles

NEXT TIME you go from Godalming to the A3 at Jackson's Corner, pause for a moment and look to the right just above the new bridge and you will see a path that leads up to the remains of Westbury barn. It was burned down soon after I gave up farming this land and now all that remains are the foundations and the granary. I still think fondly of it when I remember the sunny afternoon of that brief meeting.

It was hot and probably early in summer. I had a cart up there and was leaning against it having a breather when I looked round to see an old man with a broad brimmed hat slowly coming up the path from the Godalming road. As it is a public footpath I didn't pay any heed and waited until he came up to where I was standing when he smiled and said 'Good-day'. He was a small brown nut of a man, old but very active; indeed before I could say any more he had levered himself up on to the cart, settled himself and was lighting his pipe.

He started talking generalities about the weather and immediately betrayed a strong Australian accent. I asked him where he came from.

'Brisbane,' he replied. 'You might say I built Brisbane,' he laughed and added that sixty-five years in the building trade in the capital of Queensland entitled him to boast a bit.

'All carpentry really,' he said. 'Wooden houses on legs to keep the air circulating and some distance from the poisonous spiders and snakes.'

He then followed with the size of Brisbane; how it was the biggest city in the world if you measured size by the number of square miles covered. I was duly impressed. I noticed that he kept turning on the cart and looking at the barn.

I thought he was interested in it because it was timber-framed although I couldn't imagine it being like anything that you might find in Australia. I asked him if he would like to see inside.

He said, 'No thank you, I just wanted to look at it.'

So we both sat on the cart looking at the barn; he gently nodding his head as he did so and I wondering what his interest could be.

'I had to come and see it for the last time,' he said. I just sat there waiting.

'Would you like to hear why I came to see your barn or are you too busy?' I assured him that I was only too pleased to take a break on a hot day.

He slowly re-filled his pipe, leant against the ladder of the cart and began.

'I was a boy of fourteen, that's just seventy years ago – the old Queen still had some years to run – when I used to come to this barn. My father was a "chippy" at the builders down there,' and he pointed down to Jackson's Corner.

'We lived in Compton in a small cottage.'

'Did you help on the farm up here then?' I asked.

'My word, no,' he said. 'It was a girl.' Then he looked at me very straight and said, 'Do you know, I've never told another living soul what I'm going to tell you.'

I began to feel uncomfortable, afraid he was going to confess something. However, he was obviously determined to tell me so I kept quiet and he went on, all the while looking at the barn.

'She was a Puttenham lass, my own age, as pretty as a flower. If anyone tells you that the young don't love each other just as much as their elders, I can tell them different. This lass and I really were very fond of each other and once a week we used to meet in this barn – sort of neutral ground between the two villages. We talked, we held hands – I don't remember us kissing – perhaps we did. It was all so perfect that nothing,' and the old man became quite emphatic, 'nothing has been like it since. I mean in the way of being completely happy.' The old man's voice was now as though he was talking to himself. 'We were young, we were innocent and we were in love.'

Suddenly he remembered I was there. 'Well, of course, it ended,' and then I was afraid he would say no more, but he began again.

'Yes, each Saturday we would meet and one or other of us – we hadn't much money – would buy a bottle of ginger beer. You perhaps don't remember when it came in stone bottles with the little ball inside as a stopper? Well we would share the ginger beer – perhaps we did this instead of kissing – and when we had finished it I would shin up the beams of the barn and put them in a row as a sort of permanent record of

our meeting and sharing. You'd think we would take them back and get the penny on them but no, those bottles were really important to us. We used to look up at them and laugh – in those days we used to laugh about anything and everything.

'As I said, it ended. One Saturday – on a day not unlike today, I had bought the bottle and was unhappy because I didn't know how to tell her. My father had been in and out of work and had decided to emigrate to Australia under the old Empire scheme. I was too young to have any say – no one would have listened. In the end I told my lass straight out what was going to happen. At first I thought she was going to say something but she didn't. She just turned to me and began to cry and cry. Man, I never thought a human body could have so many tears to give out.

'She wept till it began to show on her dress. I tried to cheer her up but she just sobbed with the big tears rolling down her cheeks. In the end, half in fun, I began to catch the tears in the ginger beer bottle – she let me press the thick rim into her cheek and the tears just fell in. Cry, it was terrible. Quite suddenly she took the bottle, kissed it and gave it back to me and before I could say anything she was gone, running like the wind, back down across the field to Puttenham and I never saw her again. I put the bottle with the others – it was all I could do.

'We emigrated almost immediately to Australia, where things were even worse than here, and my parents were very unhappy. I eventually left them in Perth and I worked my way to the east. I wrote to the lass in Puttenham but never got a reply and it's only now on my first visit back to the old country that I found out she died a short time ago. No, she never married – I did – but she never did. Pretty as a picture – such a waste. Don't let anyone tell you that the young don't have feelings that matter,' he added as he slipped down from the cart.

'I must be on my way – I've the boat train to catch for back home.' Even then he seemed reluctant to leave.

'My she was a pretty lass. I wonder if the bottles are still there?'

I said, 'Would you like to have a look?'

'No,' he said. 'After all this time I wouldn't know where to look; anyway probably someone found them and claimed the pennies back. Goodbye, my friend, thank you for letting me have a sight of the old barn,' and he strode off down the path and out of my life.

Well, I did look half-heartedly around the beams next time I was in the barn; but it was a big place and like the old man I felt that they had probably gone after seventy years. A few years later I was trying to replace two tiles that had slipped near the eaves. Looking down from the ladder from outside I saw them – a neat row of a dozen stone ginger beer bottles, all with the name facing into the barn, sitting there on the plate beam that ran round the walls. I took the bottle at the end of the row, THIS IS THE ONE, and tipped it into my hand. Some clear liquid fell into my palm; of course the rain had got into it where the tiles had slipped but you know when I put my tongue to it to taste it, I swear it was salty – just slightly.

Saint Roch and the sixpence

Saint Roch and the sixpence

I AM LARGELY indebted for this story to a lady, Miss Grigson, who although dead for some years, many in Puttenham will have known. She was sacristan and some of you will perhaps remember her quietly walking up to the church in the evening to prepare the hangings and vestments for the following day's services.

She lived at a very narrow point in the Street, Jasmine Cottage, now owned by David Winter, and it was while I was held up there one day in the car that she leant over the gate to ask me in her quiet voice, 'Do you know anything about Saint Roch?'

I admitted that I knew nothing about Saint Roch but said that I would find out what I could. I was just about to ask her what it was that she particularly wanted to know when a hoot from behind told me I was blocking the road. So I went on my way hoping that I would remember the saint's name and wondering where I could get the information. I am, I fear, not too good on saints except, of course, for Saint Anthony, without whom I would never find anything; but even he is no good on the golf course where he seems totally disinterested in finding those wretched little balls.

I turned to the *Encyclopaedia Brittanica* and sure enough there was Saint Roch. I was relieved that I would have something to pass on and so I jotted down all the essentials. How Saint Roch was born about 1295 at Montpellier in France. How on the death of his parents in his twentieth year he gave all his substance to the poor. And how he is specially invoked against the plague. He received from God the favour, in return for what amounted to martyrdom, that all plague-stricken persons calling on his name should be healed. I also learnt that his cult spread through Spain, France, Germany, Belgium and Italy – no mention of Britain.

So, armed with my brief notes, the next time we met I reeled them off. The good lady, and she was good, patiently waited until I was finished and then said quietly that she knew all that. What she really wanted to know, and I clearly had not heard her question on our first meeting, was did I know anything about Saint Roch and Puttenham? I said I did not think so, but could she leave it with me?

'No hurry at all,' came the answer. 'Any time will do.'

I really thought that the answer would be 'No'; that Saint Roch was in no way connected with Puttenham and yet at the back of my mind there was something half-remembered. I searched and researched and at last I found it. I fancy I came on it after one of my free consultations with Saint Anthony, who perhaps felt a certain prejudice in favour of a measure of revelation. There it was; one line in an out-of-date, out-of-print, guide to Puttenham Church based on Mr Gosling's notes published in the 1950s during the benefice of the Reverend Philip Gaze. The one line said and I quote, 'An image of Saint Roch was given in 1503 by Stephen Burden.'

I was rather pleased with myself when I next met Miss Grigson and told her what I had found. To my surprise she seemed quite upset, perhaps put out would be more like it. All she said as her grey-blue eyes looked straight back at me was 'Extraordinary, quite extraordinary – are you sure?'

I said I felt the information was probably authentic. I mean, why should anyone bother to invent it?

She agreed and asked, 'I wonder what happened to the statue?'

I said I could find nothing about that and suggested that the numerous Cromwellians billeted in these parts during the Civil War had broken it as they generally seem to have done to that sort of image. Miss Grigson wandered off murmuring, 'Extraordinary – quite extraordinary.'

A few weeks later I approached her, saying that she might like to share what she knew about Saint Roch after the bits of information I had given her. Well, no, not quite as baldly as that, but I left her in no doubt that I was interested. She waited a moment then said, 'Come to tea next Thursday, Nellie is going to be away.' Nellie Clarke was her companion.

So next Thursday we sat down in the pleasant little sitting room of her cottage and after the smallest sandwiches I've ever tried to make into two bites she told me what had happened in Puttenham church late one evening in the middle of the previous August.

'Yes it was late,' she began, 'rather later than usual. I had put on the lights in the vestry but the rest of the church was still light enough. I was busy arranging things for Sunday, vessels and vestments and all that when I heard the church door open and somebody coming in. They closed the door behind them. I went on doing what I had to do, and then thought that perhaps I ought to put on the main church lights in case a visitor was wanting to look around. Imagine my surprise when I went into the chancel and then down into the nave to find no one there. I knew they hadn't left because, as you know if you are late for church, in no way can you open and shut Puttenham church door without everyone knowing.' I knew just what she meant.

'Well,' she continued, 'I thought perhaps some child was hiding and as I wanted to lock the church up for the night I looked down some of the pews. Just then I heard a murmur coming from behind the organ and I felt I must see if someone was taken ill or something. I forced myself to go in behind the organ and there to my surprise was a man kneeling straight on the floor praying towards the far left corner.

'As I made to come away and leave him in peace he got up stiffly and crossed himself. I felt I had disturbed him by prying so I suggested he would be more comfortable in a pew with a hassock. He looked at me in the half light and I could just see he was smiling gently.

' "No, I've finished," he said, "I come to pray to Saint Roch on occasions to thank him for favours during the great sickness. He was all we had, you know".' Miss Grigson paused in her story; and I just sat there wondering.

I broke the silence quietly and asked her, 'Did you ask him why he was praying to something that wasn't there?'

'No,' she said, 'it didn't seem any of my business.'

'Did you you ask him what sickness? Was it the influenza epidemic of 1918?'

No, she hadn't asked anything; he left her with a polite 'Good evening' but she added, she didn't feel he was old enough to have been more than a child in 1918.

We sat there in silence; I felt somehow disappointed. There was so much that could have been asked about Saint Roch. Miss Grigson suddenly broke through my reverie and regret.

'I've been doing a little bit of research myself. I found this in the present guidebook to the church.' And she quoted, 'In 1603 the register has this cryptic remark in the margin, "at this time the pestilence was very rife".'

I said to Miss Grigson, 'You are not suggesting that this sickness the man refers to had anything to do with a plague of Elizabeth I's? I mean to say!'

She answered very patiently, 'I don't know what I mean or what it all means but what I didn't tell you was that after he had said "Good evening" the stranger had walked to the back of the church and dropped a coin in the collecting box on the wall. One of my jobs is to empty the collecting box on Saturday nights. I do it as a matter of routine before going home. There were probably a dozen or so coins in the box and I scooped them out without thinking before taking them back to the vestry safe so I shall never know who put this one in.'

She handed me an Elizabethan silver coin, dated quite clearly 1591.

Some years later before she left Puttenham, Miss Grigson gave me the coin – an Elizabethan sixpence piece. Every time I handle it I say to myself, 'Extraordinary – quite extraordinary.'

By the way, Saint Roch's saint's day is August 16th, just about the date when the stranger was last seen in Puttenham.

The bells and my friend Mabel

The bells and my friend Mabel

I REALLY WAS surprised when I woke up one morning and found a completely strange young woman just an arm's length away. This had never happened to me before and I do hope you believe me. It was even more unusual since I clearly remember going to bed with Albert next door. He was from Godalming and I had known him for years behind the counter at the ironmongers. Albert bore no resemblance to my new young lady; besides being three times her age, he was rather plain and had a frightening bronchial complaint which caused him to search for breath in long repetitive gasps. Albert, frankly, was old, ugly and very poorly. His replacement was young, pretty and sleeping like a baby.

Of course, none of this would have happened but for the trend in our new hospitals of mixing up the sexes, especially in the observation wards. The nurses also had a habit of giving out sleeping pills and then shifting you about in the middle of the night. I had woken up once during just such a commotion to find myself shooting along Millbridge Ward with a young nurse using my bed as a scooter with one foot on the bottom bar. It had felt like the start of the Two Man Bob on the Cresta Run.

Anyway, Albert had gone, replaced by this pleasant looking young lady who rather intrigued me because she appeared quite well, compared with the rest of us. I never did discover why she was in; and you are right, it was none of my business. But I did wish she would wake up as I had no one to talk to, at least not as nice looking as her.

Eventually, in the middle of the afternoon she woke up. The first thing she saw was me and I've got to admit that now she did not look quite so well. Dismay spread over her face and then panic. She seemed to put on ten years as she gazed around. Her reaction at waking up to find someone of the opposite sex in the next bed was a bit disappointing.

We just had time to introduce ourselves and comment on the heat when in swept Cheesy. Had there been water in the ward she would have left a great bow wave; she was built that way. Cheesy was the sister in charge of us and she took her job seriously yet cheerfully; her smile disguised a quiet determination to make us conform. We all liked her, I think.

Cheesy was very Welsh, indeed she got her nickname from the one word reply she gave to anyone who asked where she came from, 'Caerphillynearcardiffofcourse'. We respected her because she was good at her job but I am afraid she considered us objects that made the place untidy. Thinking about it now, perhaps Cheesy was right; we were a scruffy lot.

On this occasion, she only said one word and that was to me, and I knew exactly what she meant.

'Legs,' she said and went out. Obeying immediately, I uncrossed my legs. Apparently it was bad for the circulation to lie with crossed legs and as we were on top of our beds due to the extreme heat we were easy targets for Cheesy's attention. It was the beginning of a friendly little battle between us. It seems rather trivial now but long hours with not much to do taught you to grasp at any diversion to fill the day. I felt that next time I had a chance I would question Cheesy just for fun. Meanwhile I was busy trying to find out about Mabel, whose name by now had appeared on the board above her bed.

Our conversation to begin with centred round her family, husband, children and the like and assumed no particular interest until I mentioned that I came from Puttenham.

'That's the place with the bells, isn't it?'

I agreed that the church had got a peel of bells but by the tone of her question or look in her face I saw that she knew quite a bit about Puttenham and that its bells were important to her. We left it at that for the moment, and talked about other things.

Later I decided to find out more about Mabel and her connection with my home base and was just about to bring up the subject when Cheesy appeared. She said nothing but took both my feet and separated them forcibly, as inadvertently I had crossed them. Now was my chance.

'Sister,' I said, 'have you ever been to Westminster Abbey?'

'Why?' came the answer.

'Because,' I said, 'the people on the tombs there have done pretty well for themselves and all their legs are crossed.'

She just grunted and stalked off. I felt that was a round to me, although I knew it was not the end of the matter. Cheesy was not so easily defeated. Anyway I decided to obey orders,

keep my feet apart and avoid interruptions so that I could find out why Mabel was interested in Puttenham and especially why she had mentioned the bells.

Eventually, without wanting to appear too nosy, I found out that Mabel's family had lived in Puttenham somewhere in the Street. Just where was a bit obscure because they had moved when Mabel was a baby.

'I'm not sure where it was,' she said, 'but I do know that it wasn't far from the church because my mum always told me that but for Puttenham church and its bells I wouldn't be alive today.'

Mabel said all this quite quietly and sincerely and I had no reason to doubt her. As you can imagine I was intrigued. Just as I was going to ask more, Cheesy was with us again.

'You know these fellows in this Westminster Abbey of yours?'

I was now regretting that I had ever mentioned the place.

'Have you ever thought that perhaps they wouldn't have ended up there if they hadn't been stupid and kept their legs crossed? Just remember that boyo.' And she swept away triumphantly.

I returned to Mabel and the bells. The explanation was really quite reasonable and memorable. Mabel had been upstairs in her cot, her mother downstairs dozing in front of the fire half listening to bell-ringing practice. Her mother liked the bells and knew a bit about it from her father who had been a bell ringer at one time. It was a bitterly cold December night and the rounds they were ringing sounded clearly in the sharp chill air.

Suddenly there was a crash of bells; the steady measured rhythm was broken by one bell that rang repeatedly out of time with the others. It went on ringing, getting slower long after the others had stopped until it finally died away. The break in the rhythm and the silence which followed was enough to rouse Mabel's mother and for no apparent reason she felt a need to check on her baby daughter. When she found her she was silently choking to death; she had already gone blue. According to Mabel, her mother picked her up by the feet, smacked her bottom and she coughed up a button she had sucked off her clothes. Her mother never forgot the bells that woke her and indeed at the time took the trouble to find out that it was a broken bell-rope that caused the crashing sound which roused her.

Shortly after telling me this Mabel was moved and I've never seen her since. It was only when I was talking to my wife Esther about Mabel and the bells that she reminded me we had both been there. She remembered that night in the bell-tower when Fred Turvil led on the Number One; Esther was on Two; Mrs Hurcomb, the butcher's wife, was ringing

Number Three; I was on Four and Stanley Hobbs on the Tenor. Charles Avenell was on the fateful Number Five bell whose rope broke and saved the life of my friend Mabel – such a pleasant person to meet and, dare I say it, to wake up alongside.

Madame Agréable

Madame Agréable

MY AUNT and her harmonium were both very French. I first remember them before the war when I, in my teens, was visiting during holidays. They seemed then to be inseparable. My aunt, a kindly person, was musical and played the organ in the village church above La Ciotat on the Côte d'Azur where she lived. She had a delightful way of giving personalities to the things about her house. The wood-burning stove to heat the water was 'Monsieur Comfortable' and her harmonium was 'Madame Agréable' and it did indeed make an agreeable sound.

My aunt would have the choir down from the village for practice around Madame Agréable and that was where Marie comes in. In 1936 she was perhaps twelve or thirteen years old and I thought her striking even then. She had long black hair, startlingly lively eyes and a perfect complexion. She sang beautifully too, which endeared her to my aunt, who was, incidentally, quite amused by my interest in choir practice.

The war came to the south coast of France; although only

briefly a battleground there were a number of German troops stationed there for most of those long years. Civilians suffered at the hands of the French police who took their orders from the Gestapo. My uncle, who was English and a sick man, was arrested and imprisoned on a trumped-up charge; he was returned to my aunt two days before he died. The treatment or lack of it had been too much for him. That is a story all of its own.

So when I went back to La Ciotat immediately after the war, things had changed, the place and the people were scarred. However, Monsieur Comfortable, the stove, still worked and the children were coming down again from the village to stand around Madame Agréable for choir practice. But no Marie; I remember so well looking for her sweet face among the choir. My aunt gave some reason, such as Marie's interest now being more in the café-tabac in the village than in the church. Without too much delay I started going with my aunt up the steep climb to the village where she played. After a few times I saw Marie again. She was nine years older and more striking than ever with a bevy of admirers whom I soon joined. They were nice young people, full of fun, all anxious to make up for the wasted years of the war.

What time I was allowed by my aunt I spent with Marie and her circle; though no one would explain to me why she now wore a black glove on her left hand. I asked one of the others about it and was quite quickly given to understand that this was something that Marie and her friends did not want to talk about. Hard as I tried, I found it difficult not to keep glancing at it and wondering if the third and fourth fingers were missing or deformed or curled up inside the glove.

My aunt was equally uninformative, adopting the French ploy that has no English equivalent of shrugging the shoulders, spreading the hands, pouting the lips and saying absolutely nothing. I was left just wondering about the black glove.

During these weeks the curé of the church where my aunt played came down to discuss the services with her. I got to know him and to like him. He seemed young for a curé and rather unusual. I say that because, although he was good at his work and loved by his parishioners, he had a modernistic side to him that did not seem in keeping with the fusty, musty, stifling atmosphere of his dark and dank old church. The first time I saw him he was tinkering with his motorcycle, an old BSA with a Villiers engine, of which he was very proud, having kept it going through the war. He was crouched over his bike; his thick powerful neck quite red in the sun. He was a 'ginger man'; the hairs on the back of his hands shone brightly as he tinkered. He would take me, sitting pillion, for rides round the country with frequent retuning stops if he didn't feel he was getting the maximum from his machine. He was not just machine mad; he had a wisdom of which I wish I had a better record. Like good sermons, if you don't write down what is said, they are soon forgotten. Just one piece of his thinking has stayed with me not only for its good sense but because it reflected the character and interests of the man.

I commented one day while we were talking about the war that I could not understand a God who would allow such horrors to happen. His reply came slowly.

'I don't understand Him either.'

Then he quickly asked, 'Do you know Groucho Marx?' I nodded and he went on, 'Groucho one day applied to join a club which turned him down, "blackballed" as you say in English. Groucho's only comment was that it was just as well as he wouldn't want to belong to a club that let in people like him.'

The curé went on, 'By the same token, I don't want to understand a God that somebody like me can understand – He wouldn't be much good.'

On one of our trips I took courage and asked the curé about Marie and the black glove.

'It's quite simple,' he said, 'she cut off the ends of two fingers to defend herself and anyone who says it was an accident is a malicious liar.'

His usual good humour lapsed for a moment and he grew quite vehement.

'Marie is a good girl, a very honourable person.'

His remonstrance came across with less pomposity in French. I tried to reassure him that I fully respected her virtue but could he tell me more?

'Yes,' he replied, 'I don't see why you should not know the truth.' He then repeated that it was quite simple and he unfolded what had happened on that awful day.

As the war was dragging to its close the discipline of the German troops, who were either old or very young, was faltering. One evening Marie was working in her father's butchers shop on her own when four German soldiers surprised her as she was chopping meat. They were very young and rather drunk. Marie feared they were going to molest her and so she threatened to cut off her fingers if they didn't leave her alone. They would not believe her and in their oafish way came towards her. She carried out her threat. The soldiers left in horror; one was sick on the way out. The curé and I drove home and never mentioned Marie again.

The idyllic weeks in the sun came to an end. I returned to England and forgot the curé, Marie and her black glove and just occasionally communicated with my aunt.

A full eight years later I went back with my family to stay at La Ciotat. My aunt, who seemed in those days to be immortal, was still busy with Madame Agréable and the choir but seemed unwilling to talk about Marie and the old days. At first it was just the shrugging shoulders ploy and then gradually I discovered by cajolery that Marie was not in my aunt's good books. From others I managed to find out that she was now married and living in a long dull village on the road to Aix en Provence. We had to pass it on the way home and so parking the family at a craft shop where the local coppersmith was beating out pots I went, for old time's sake, to have a look for Marie.

It was not difficult to find her – she and her husband had a small garage. I recognised her at once with pleasure. She was a little worn and tired but still very handsome; however at first she reacted in a way that made me wish I hadn't bothered to look for her.

'Oh no – Oh my God,' and her left hand flew to her throat; the black glove had been abandoned and for the first time I saw the fingers cut short. Then suddenly she became resigned, reconciled somehow, and she called me over to the trellis of the garden fence where she said simply and quietly, 'Look – my husband and my son.'

There in the yard was the former curé as I first remember him, crouching over a machine, his neck as red and powerful as ever; a little boy alongside as ginger as his father.

'Are you happy, Marie?' I asked.

'Beyond belief,' she replied, 'although sometimes we are haunted by the past.'

She smiled and we said 'Goodbye' and I have taken the hint and never been back.

My aunt and her harmonium moved to England, where they lived at Berthorpe, the home of my late mother-in-law Clarice Tuckwell. They were happy there for some years. My aunt died, in her tidy way, on the last day of 1970. Her harmonium, Madame Agréable, which has such memories for me, is known to most of you. After some vicissitudes, she now sits proudly on the right-hand side of the chancel in Wanborough Church – promoted from being just a harmonium for choir practice – and has become a church organ in her own right.

Since writing this Madame Agréable has been replaced at Wanborough by a modern electronic rival and has accepted retirement with my son, Adam, on the outskirts of Ashburton in Devon.

Special places

Special places

PERHAPS it's more a bit of local history than a mystery; that is if you don't count the missing schoolmaster. You would understand it easily if you were an Australian aborigine or a Liverpool football fan. I am talking about respect for special places; the aborigine with his deference for sacred trees and stones; the fan who finds solace in the corner of Anfield where the magic feet of Dalglish play on for ever. They would understand.

Such places can be connected with people, buildings or events or they may be somewhere that just seems special. I'm not sure which kind this is. But the special place I want to share with you is not a hundred miles from here; indeed it's at the bottom of the steps up to the church at the corner of the village street that tradition has called 'Kill Priest Corner', although there is no record of anybody coming to grief there. I think it was probably called that early in the last century out of resentment at the road being re-routed by the owner of the priory, Mr Sumner, to give himself more privacy. That corner of the road is a special place for me.

The war memorial is probably one good reason for its importance. I think of the forty-four times I have stood there, usually in the cold, never in the rain, thinking of those I knew and whose faces are fading. We used to meet, for many years after the war, in School Lane and march, the First War veterans in the lead, up the Street to the memorial. Then the old soldiers asked if they could perhaps bring up the rear at a gentler pace and later still if they could meet us at the memorial as the hill, past the Post Office, seemed to have got steeper. Eventually we were all quite pleased to forget the marching and have now come to a halt at the corner for our few moments of remembrance. A peaceful setting for a war memorial, you might think, yet it was not always so.

The war memorial was indeed to split the village, especially the churchgoers, from top to bottom. Briefly, the controversy was over the design. All agreed that it should be a cross; but there the unanimity ended. The Rector, Canon Cooke-Yarborough, the Rector's Warden and the High Anglican party favoured a cross with a crucifix showing the body of Christ. The People's Warden, on the other hand, joined by the less high Anglicans of the congregation and a body of village opinion, thought a plain cross would be best. Of course, the battle was fought with the dignity that suited the subject. No alley-cat scratching and snarling, rather the determination of stags drawing back and charging at each other with a clash of antlers and all the consequent headaches. In the end, as you can see, the Low Church faction won. There was to be no crucifix. Then, at the last moment the Rector asked that a 'drip-stone hood mould' should be placed over where the body of Christ would have been had it been a crucifix. It was agreed and so now we have a plain cross as a war memorial with a small shelter over the top – a triumph for the losing party in the controversy? Not really. This was no concession on the part of the plain cross party; it was just that at the parochial church council meeting nobody had the courage to ask what a 'drip-stone hood mould' was that the Rector was so keen on. It all seemed so important at that time. Today there it stands, just about right, with its plain cross and 'drip-stone hood mould' on top – a typical Anglican compromise, some might say.

Events and their memory can enhance the significance of a special place; this has indeed occurred at 'Kill Priest Corner' for me. It happened on a frosty December evening sometime in the 1960s. The church, having been first mentioned in 1160, was thought due to have a birthday or eight hundred years' commemoration in 1960. We did lots of things, including restoration and redecoration and, as a finale to the year, a nativity play, which none of us who were there will forget and which has added so much to the magic of this corner for me.

The nativity scene was set in the left doorway of the barn, opposite the church. The doors were opened to reveal the crib and Holy Family in front of various curtains draped over the corn dryer that was once there.

It worked well as a setting; the kings and shepherds appearing from round the barn out of the dark. The kings were mounted on three fine horses provided by Percy Podger of Binscombe; one of them ridden by Charles Bone, the artist; the second by Bill Hayter, the publican of the Good Intent and the third by Nicky Elwes of Wanborough Manor, who drew the short straw as he had to black up as Melchior. I

can still see and hear them as they came clattering round the corner.

You might ask who and where were the audience? That was quite amazing because many more than we expected came and crowded on to the pathway in front of the barn entrance and across the road in the churchyard.

They could all hear the words as we had an address system which, although adequate for sound, was unreliable for being on or off. It was found better to leave it permanently on. The narrator was suddenly aware of a small boy who appeared and very audibly broadcast into the microphone, 'Mr Podger says, if you get the chance, put up the chestnut – he'll take anything over 200 guineas.'

The eight hundred years of the church were relived by the children who, in bunches, were launched by Jean Ford, the headmistress, out of the barn doors; each posse dressed in the period costume of a different century. A simple verse, about events in the village, was read as each of the eight centuries skipped past us. It started with the building of the church –

Yes, at last it's begun at the top of the Street
The children run out – their feet
Tread the base and leave small prints
In the soft white chalk between the flints.

And the children wait and a century goes
And the children play as the tower grows.
Up goes a spire with a wrought-iron spike
While the boys fish Cutt Mill Ponds for pike.

Up the tower and look down's the game,
Counting the pilgrims as they came.
And the children turned – I can hear them call,
'My – doesn't the Street look small.'

And the children grew and the church grew
With chancel, windows, porch and pew.
And the Black Death passed by Wanborough way
'The Puttenham air's too pure' they say.

And a century of lovers up Lascombe Lane
Forget the wait, forgive the rain,
They see the clock with its new gold hands
And think of the parson calling banns.

Down the Street the thick thatch flames,
The young forget their conker games.
The jackdaws black against the fire
And the blaze brings down the arrow spire.

And I see in your church your women weep,
For the men and boys the wars keep,
Each heart in shade without the light
Of the men that should be here tonight.

It is difficult now to recall completely the beauty of it all; the joyful haphazard nature of local people doing a very local thing. For instance, the shepherds, headed by Ron Ford and my son Simon, who like the rest were un-rehearsed, seeking to control fully grown ewes caught suddenly in the flood-lights and surrounded by people. They took off for darkness and were not seen again.

The last word, literally, was given to the Angel Gabriel at the top of the tower, standing on an orange box behind the low parapet. There stood the white figure, with the gold wings created by Faith Winter, swaying gently in the evening breeze. It was Eric Roberts, the deputy headmaster, who found the unaccustomed weight of the wings caused his unsteadiness, though some of the less charitable put it down to the chill of the night air and the need for supplementary compensation in liquid form. Eric was a friendly, convivial sort of fellow whom everyone liked and I relish now the strong Welsh accent he gave to the 'in secula seculorum' which finished our play.

I will leave you with a mystery which comes back to me as

I think of this special bit of Puttenham. What did happen to Eric Roberts? He did his work here and was rewarded by promotion to the headship of Shere School. His last known act, some years later, was to take his car to the edge of the cliffs overlooking Cardigan Bay where he left it. He was never seen again.

What are these special places? Sometimes they are less important than my corner by the church where so much has happened. It could be just a tree on the common under which one has sheltered on a wet night. Or it might be the brow of a hill or the turning point of a path. I can explain no more and can only ask – is there a hand that touches us at such times and in such places?

William and Mary Westwood

William and Mary Westwood

I FEEL I MUST get down on paper the story of William and Mary Westwood and their son Noel before it is forgotten. Perhaps writing it may stop the sadness that comes over me each time I pass what remains of Ash Farm. It couldn't be told much earlier because until all concerned had died it might have opened up old sores and made people talk. Not that it has anything scandalous in it, nor anyone who behaved badly; rather the opposite, but still it might have caused sorrow to Noel. Now that he has gone, too, I think it is worth recording.

It's really a very simple story. I've always felt its poignancy because it occurred so close to where I live and although I met only one of the three people involved, I have known the background, and indeed the farm where it happened, most of my life. The details, such as they are, came from neighbours and old friends and although I doubt if I've got it all right, it's probably as near the truth as anything, bearing in mind that Noel, even fifty years later, never had much to say.

Only once was I bold enough to ask how he felt about it

after all these years. He just lent on his stick, looked into the fire and then looked down at his boots and said resentfully, 'Dad shouldn't have done it. It were wrong, very wrong.'

Lying just east of the village, Ash Farm was at that time about sixty acres of not very good greensand. It has gone now as a farm, some of it for council houses and the rest taken by neighbouring farmers, as has happened all round these parts.

William and Mary went in as tenants in about 1890 at ten shillings an acre, which was considered quite a high rent, for agriculture at the time was in the doldrums, with imports from Canada and the States and the new freezer ships starting to bring lamb from New Zealand. But the Westwoods worked hard and I understand that William was a great hand with horses and that his ploughing was as near perfection as may be. They survived and, indeed, prospered, at a difficult time.

William was a quiet strong man, who kept himself to himself, but whose advice, especially on horses, was much sought after locally. He is still remembered by a few for the quiet way he broke and gentled his horses. George Tremblett, the carter from Down Ashton, recalls, 'Billy Westwood was always kind and slow in his breaking. He had no fear; it's people that have fear that are hard on horses.'

When he ploughed, William whistled the same three notes hour by hour; it was just his way.

He didn't like machinery; he never really took to the binder that he bought when they came in. His pleasure was the single-furrow two-horse plough which needed just the one double-ended spanner; one end for the share bolts and the big end to adjust the knife coulter. To the plough he tied this

plough spud with its flat end and long wooden handle which he used to scrape the mould boards. I got that when the farm was finally sold up and it hangs over my fireplace to this day. It's not much to remember William by – apart, that is, from what he did in 1918.

Mary is remembered in some ways better than William because in most villages the women seem to live longer, and a few old friends can still recall her ways. The school mistress, Miss Gideon, who retired to Bexhill, wrote a long letter about those early days. She had quite a turn of phrase, that was probably why she was asked to do the Nature Notes in the parish magazine.

'Mary Westwood,' she wrote, 'was a busy, friendly woman full of warmth; inside I think she had a copper kettle she was mentally burnishing and the quiet radiance of her business shone out through short-sighted eyes and pink cheeks.' Just how well Miss Gideon knew Mary I don't know, nor indeed to what extent they were friends.

Mary gave birth to Noel on Christmas Day 1900 – the date

is important and not just because she insisted on him being called Noel, a name that William found difficult. He would have rather called the child William like himself and his father before him.

Name or no, William loved his boy very much, of that there can be no doubt; not that he said much about it. Only once did he tell Mary, when he was later trying to explain that just the sight of the boy hurt him. He banged his chest when he told her and couldn't say much more.

In March 1918 this strong love made William walk into Guildford to volunteer for the Royal West Surrey Regiment. You see, Noel was coming up to be eighteen at Christmas, when he would get his call-up papers. William knew that if he joined up himself, Noel would be considered essential back home on the farm and so exempted from conscription.

Both Mary and Noel protested and said it was a young man's job and that he was too old. William, only just forty, said this was nonsense and why should the young die clearing up the troubles made by the last generation? The rector had a go at him too, saying that God had given his Son to save the world, and that was the way it was.

William replied, and I know this upset the rector, that he never understood how God could have given his Son knowing He was to be killed if He really loved Him.

'He can't have felt like I do about Noel.'

The rector tried to explain about redemption but William couldn't make much of that.

After a short time in Stoughton Barracks, William went to France, leaving Mary and the boy to run the farm. He was killed while grooming the colonel's horse by a heavy howitzer fired miles away. They found him lying across the neck of the horse, both killed by the same shell.

When I take down the plough spud and run my hand along the old holly handle, gone like ivory now with the WW burnt in, I can't help feeling what a pity it all was and what a waste. Had William waited, he need never have gone, for the war was to end in November and with it conscription. Noel would never have been called up, anyway, for his eighteenth birthday, if you remember, was not till Christmas Day, a full six weeks after the armistice and peace.

'No, it was more auburn'

'No, it was more auburn'

THE LAST time I went by train, apart from trips to London, was when I went up to York some years ago. I was going alone and if I have to travel that way I have two hopes; one, that I find a good book to enjoy and the other, that I am left in peace. I found a good book – a P. G. Wodehouse. Settled down in my corner seat I was just content to follow the doings at Blandings Castle with occasional glances out of the window and perhaps the odd wink of sleep.

Most of the time, however, I read, knowing that the chance of being disturbed was slight as it was an express that only stopped twice. First stop Grantham, the magic of my peaceful journey was broken when the carriage door was flung open and in piled a family with luggage, umbrellas and children everywhere. I shifted slightly to make room for them and without undue haste tried to get back to my P. G. Wodehouse. I did not want to appear unwelcoming in any way but I was, I must admit, sorry that they had picked on my carriage.

They were the average British family; father, mother and 1.8 children. The little boy, I soon realised, the .8, being only partially connected to the human race. He was sat next to me and kept thumping the seat with the backs of his legs. His sister, by all appearances, was completely normal and a nice child. The mother, an older edition of her daughter, had an open, kind face; I instinctively liked her. The father was different. I knew that he was going to come between me and my Wodehouse.

It was not that he was unpleasant – far from it – he was friendly; but I knew he would want to talk. He had a face that I can't in any way remember; it was so covered up with paraphernalia. His cap came down to meet his heavy horn-rimmed spectacles, where they stopped began a big bushy moustache; a huge curly pipe with a china bowl like a hand-basin covered the rest of his face. He said he liked meeting people and talking to them and finding out all about them. At first, he told me all about himself, none of which can I recall. Then came the fateful words, 'and where do you hail from?' At this his wife suggested that perhaps I wanted just to read my book; I had folded the Penguin on my knee. The husband said there was always time to read – 'anyway the gentleman was not reading a proper book'. I felt that only Jeeves would have an answer to that.

I felt safe now because although our delightful village is important to those who live here, it has rarely been heard of by outsiders. So I trotted out that I came from a small village called Puttenham. 'You'll not have heard of it,' I said, confidently. That is where I made my mistake.

'Puttenham, of course I know Puttenham. Don't we Mildred?' Her face had gone quite grey; she suddenly looked miserable yet resigned.

'Don't look like that Mildred,' he said, 'you don't come out of it too well, I know, but we must tell the gentleman what happened to us at Puttenham.'

At this his wife turned away and looked out of the train window – my heart went out to her; but I think we both knew that nothing would stop him now. And if truth be known, I was just the slightest bit intrigued, if only because I had run into somebody who knew Puttenham.

He began convincingly anyway.

'We stopped,' he said, 'at a pub in the middle of the village. I went in and had a drink. Mildred sat in the car – she doesn't drink.'

I thought, uncharitably, I wonder how many wives don't drink just so they may have a few minutes of peace?

'The landlord was a big bluff old boy,' he continued. That must have been Ted Edwards at the Good Intent

'I asked him where we could stop the night with the caravan, that wasn't too far away. It was generally agreed round the bar that we could not do better than to turn right and go on to some ponds.'

I immediately recognised these as being Cutt Mill Ponds when the man said that they were only a couple of miles down the road and had drawn their caravan on to a flat sandy bit near water.

'As soon as we had got things set up Mildred said that if I would like to go for a walk she would cook the supper. It was getting dusky so I pushed off for my walk straight away. I went along that first pond and then I turned a bit and saw

another stretch of water through the trees lying back towards the right.'

At this point, he suggested, that it would perhaps help if he drew a map. I said that it was not necessary and that I knew where it was that he was talking about. 'That's the General's Pond,' I said.

'Well,' he continued, 'I sat down on an old tree stump to light my pipe and suddenly,' here he paused a moment and watched me closely, 'I saw a ghost. Do you believe in ghosts?'

I replied that I was a bit ambivalent about them, having never seen one. He looked doubtful and went on, 'Well, you do or you don't, I don't know. I didn't believe in them but I do now. I swear that I saw a ghost as certain as I'm sitting here.'

His wife shrunk into her corner seat; her eyes were tightly shut now but too tight for her to be asleep. It seemed as if she would give anything to be anywhere but on that train listening to him telling all this to a stranger.

'I tell you,' he went on, 'she was a tall red-haired lady of about thirty-five to forty, with a long old-fashioned dress. She had a very sad face – I can see it plainly. She was really near – just a few feet away, and I could see right through her.' He looked a bit embarrassed by this last claim.

'Yes, it's true – I could see the bushes right through her; she was dripping wet – the water kept on running off her as if she was coming out of water the whole time.'

'Then a funny thing happened,' he went on. 'To begin with, you see, I wasn't at all afraid – just surprised. I suddenly felt she was trying to tell me something. "Get back quickly," she seemed to say. "Get back." I suddenly felt panic; you know ghosts are supposed to fade away or something. Well as far as I know this one didn't – I left her. As I got back to the van I could see clouds of blue smoke. Yes, there were, Mildred.' He ignored the fact that his wife's eyes were shut, and continued, 'She had let the fat catch alight and there was a regular little fire going.'

Clearly he was getting to the most important part of his story; I could tell that by the long pause before he started again.

'I'm not one to boast, but in an emergency I'm at my best. I dashed down to the pond with a bucket – I soon had the fire out. But when people say they don't believe in ghosts I always tell them how one saved my Mildred and the kids; I always tell them that.'

I just caught Mildred's head nodding in agreement.

'Yes,' he added laughing, 'it's one of my best stories and

what's funny is that you are the first person I have told it to who knows the place it happened.'

I felt it was funny too; but not hilarious. The possible interest of the story had been spoilt for me by the obvious misery of the man's wife.

Shortly after that I said goodbye to my average British family at the second stop on the way to York. After they piled out of the carriage and left me in peace I found it difficult to get back to Blandings Castle, because although the man had been a talkative bore he appeared sincere. If anyone has ever seen a ghost I think he would qualify. I felt disturbed by the whole episode.

I came home two or three days later and more as a piece of quiet conversation I told the story to my wife, Esther, and her mother. My late mother-in-law Clarice Tuckwell, a forthright lady, said she thought it was all nonsense; she didn't believe in ghosts. She paused then stopped knitting for a moment. I can see her now, knitting in that Continental way, taught by a Belgian nanny I believe, in which the needles are manoeuvred round the work in an angular awkward style instead of the flowing English style of my own mother. For my mother-in-law to stop knitting meant that she was really thinking about something important.

'Of course, I don't believe a word of it,' she said, 'but I must say it is rather extraordinary – especially there at the General's Pond.'

Then she told us about Cecilia Howard of Hampton Lodge.

'It's a long time ago,' she began, 'soon after the First War. I suppose Cecilia was about my age – perhaps a bit older. We were friends, she and I. Well, it all started in the old school at

Puttenham, at what was called a penny concert – you know, singing, recitations and occasional talks. Cecilia asked that night to give a recitation – a thing she had never done before. She recited the whole of Thomas Hood's "The Bridge of Sighs", tears streaming down her face as she spoke.'

It's all there in the *Oxford Book of English Verse*; a long poem with the theme of a young girl, unfortunately wronged, who drowns herself. I quote:

Take her up tenderly,
Lift her with care;
Fashion'd so slenderly
Young, and so fair!

Look at her garments
Clinging like cerements;
Whilst the wave constantly
Drips from her clothing;
Take her up instantly,
Loving, not loathing.

My mother-in-law continued, 'We all sat in our seats as she walked through us down the hall and into School Lane. None of us followed her; I think we were all too moved to know what to do. I ought to have done something but didn't. The next day she was found floating, face upwards, in the General's Pond at Cutt Mill. She is buried in Seale.'

I went to Seale churchyard. I looked over all the main part, which is beautifully trim, without success. At last, in a rough neglected corner on the right, under beech trees that were

dripping with rain, was a flat memorial to Robert Mowbray Howard. Above it stood a little upright gravestone, nearly covered with ivy, which said simply: 'In Loving Memory Audre Cecilia 2nd wife of Robert Mowbray Howard at rest Jan 28 1926.' A place, I felt, of infinite sadness.

When the chance occurred, I remembered one thing about the lady that my talkative chap on the train had mentioned. I asked my mother-in-law if Cecilia Howard had had red hair.

'Oh no,' she said, resting her needles for a moment, 'it was more auburn.'

After a long pause, she started knitting again.

From a secret drawer

From a secret drawer

HOW THIS document came into my hands is quite simple. I found it in a desk I inherited from my aunt who lived her last years not in her native France but at Berthorpe in Puttenham Heath Road. She also left me the harmonium which now serves as the organ for Wanborough Church over the hill. The desk was provincial French of about the end of the eighteenth century, with its usual complement of rather obvious secret drawers; it was in one of these that among a jumble of old photos, newspaper cuttings, dance programmes and old paraphernalia I found this document.

That is the simple part. Who wrote it and to whom and indeed how it came into existence I just don't know. The manuscript is not even complete; the first and last pages are missing. How many there should be I am not sure as the pages are not numbered and it ends abruptly in the middle of a sentence. How much longer it was is anyone's guess. I give it to you with no theories, explanations or apologies and I can answer no questions about it because so much of it I just don't understand.

The manuscript starts '... is beginning to break a little – just occasionally the bent rays come round and I have a moment. It becomes clear for a time although I don't mean time like I used to. I could not stand more than this yet and it goes or rather I lose it knowing it is all still there. Of course when I arrived here I was a long time just in darkness. Not fearful darkness but the darkness of slowly awakening. Now it is something like the northlight from above just before dawn that I remember as a child when I was alive.

'I have all my old self and this is a burden; had I brought less with me I should be nearer than I am. I had, as you know, so many passions and selfish things – those things I used to be proud of; now I must lose them. Perhaps if I had learned to forget myself occasionally when alive it might have made it easier. We get there in the end – at least I hope so – I do hope so. At the moment I am carrying a blinding load that makes the going difficult. No one tells you much; you have to work it out for yourself and as you remember, taking thought was never my strong point.

'The most important thing I have yet to learn is silence; I mean "not talking", we make so much noise some of us. It seems we just can't lose this quickly. The chatter is everlasting; most of it justifying talk about ourselves. I'm no better than the others really but I am beginning to learn; I think it is the half-seen bent rays that are doing it.

'I really can't explain it because you will have difficulty with "X".' (This was written not with the small 'x' of school algebra but in this old typed copy capital 'X' was used).

'"X" is the other dimension which our senses – yes all of them – get when the bent rays break in. It's as if all our feeling, seeing, hearing, touching, tasting, thinking is cubed. No that's not it, because although going round is there, there is also going through as well.

'Something like it isn't unknown on earth in rather feeble form. Just once or twice it came and went.' (In the margin someone has pencilled faintly Mahler Eighth, Beethoven Emperor Concerto).

'You told me...' (here the manuscript is torn and some is lost and it continues with a new page).

'Some poor souls just can't shake off the earth life. It's sad but it doesn't last; they keep going back until they find it a waste of time which funnily enough is rather important in eternity. They are called DOGS here – I think it stands for Drab Old Ghosts and really some of the things they get up to are rather odd. No matter; they learn and are free eventually. There are a few who are not DOGS, who live a double existence for a time. They are sad, silent folk who go away and come back again, waiting. I think they have made Love-Bonds that are stronger than death. For them there is only waiting; but I have noticed they are quick to learn when the wait is over – perhaps sharing themselves has helped. They go on quickly in any case and stand the rays easier than the rest of us.

'By the way, I must tell you that mankind – us humans – have a rather different status here. We always considered ourselves so important didn't we? – here we are just a part of creation. It takes some learning and ...' (there is another break here where a page has been torn and it starts again in the middle of a sentence) '... dying to oneself again and again are we refined enough to go on. I'm getting impatient and this is supposed to be a good sign. I hope so – it's been a long journey and I have had so much to unload.

'Talking of others and their journeys I've had time to watch and wish. I'll save the wishes; but watching has shown that artists seem to learn quickly or rather quicker than the rest of us. At least artists for whom the importance was the creation and not the medium. We used to live by symbolism, similes, analogies, didn't we? – I expect you still do; well watch them carefully please – you will find them very heavy here and it is quite a business shedding them. I know you have to have them when you are alive; it's the only way to explain the inexplicable and bear the unbearable but try to mark them "not wanted on my last voyage" and come with what you can carry easily. Everything is straightforward here; no half-truths – it's all solid and real – yet I seem to miss so much. It reminds me of when we used to sit by the river together – those kingfishers – you either saw them or you didn't. So often one of us missed seeing them.

'I stood by a window the other day and the rays caught me and I know that I've got to go on. I shall not write again my dear friend. We will have to wait, although I must in truth be fair to you – I can't delay. It's like that here – but who knows where you will be and indeed that I shan't still be waiting. Alexis was waiting for me and took me by the hand. This I do promise you, that someone, and who it is may be a surprise, will be waiting for you. Keep this just for yourself and be thankful for the one who is in Love-Bond for bringing it.

'On reading this through – I know you will be asking what are those rays? The "X" factor makes it all impossible to describe but anyone who tells you that eternity is dull and not to be wanted is to be pitied – they are missing the signs. The rays are coloured but with more colours than any spectrum that you know and the music is of a range beyond your hearing. But don't imagine it's all light and music – that is just the rays – the rest beyond the rays, and I've only caught a glimpse, is so real, so incorruptible, so full of purpose that it still hurts after I've turned away. Beyond the...' (there the manuscript ends).

In Puttenham Church

In Puttenham Church

SUDDENLY he was beside me. It wasn't frightening in any sense but I was surprised because I had thought I was alone – just noseying about looking at one or two things that have always fascinated me about this place. I remember looking at the Debell slab set in the floor by the font and thinking it was just a bit too perfect. And then I went up to the tomb in the chancel on the right, done a hundred years earlier. Here was cheerful disregard of any rules though the letters were as crisp and clear as the day they were cut.

Innocent enough occupation. I was at peace with the world and myself when I saw the man was beside me bending over the slab in the chancel. He spoke slowly, as if there was endless time.

'You love this place?'

I would perhaps have expected 'like' rather than 'love' to have been the question. But no, he said 'love', so I replied quite slowly, 'Yes, I suppose you could say I love this place.'

We stood there, awkwardly for a moment and I wondered what I should say. At last, I felt I must say something.

'Does this church mean something to you then?' I asked.

'Oh yes,' he replied quickly, 'This and other places like it mean everything to me. I love it, and in particular the things in it.'

I was intrigued because I had no idea who he was; he didn't seem to be a local and I could not understand why the contents of the place should mean so much to him. He could see I was puzzled.

'The things that I love are the things that are made by men and put here.' He came down to the small window on the south side of the chancel. 'The man that put that window in seven hundred years ago is still a most important chap to me. I like the thought of his working to place it just right; the struggle he had with tools that would not stay sharp; the sadness he felt when having finished it that it did not sit quite straight; how he wished that he was better at what he did.' I could just about follow what he was talking about when he was off again, not giving me a chance to comment.

'He must be remembered – people who do things must be remembered even if we don't know their names. Names don't matter but the men that made all this for us must be thought of and thanked.'

I knew he was unstoppable and I now felt I was scarcely visible to him. He continued stroking the stone of the pillars with the back of his hand as he passed as though it was a girl's cheek. The thought of the girl's cheek gave me a chance to get back in the conversation and I asked him if he ever considered women to be of any importance in the church as a building.

'Yes,' he said. 'What they give may not be seen so often in glass and stone but shows itself in a more delicate and subtle way.'

'It's difficult,' he said and his voice dropped as he continued, 'if you had seen her and heard her as I did. The song was immortal and the notes came from beyond and have stayed forever.'

I admitted that I was lost as he went on, 'She was lovely and when she finished her song her glorious golden head hung down like a sunflower in September.' He was deeply moved.

As we passed down the aisle he regained his composure and began again quite naturally. 'Perhaps if we could understand time better we should be less careless about those who have left us so much.' I felt doubtful and anxious and it must have shown. He then said precisely and slowly what I shall never forget.

'Time is not a straight line. It's a circle and we must always be conscious of the other points in the circle as we cross them or pass them.' He could see I was not really understanding.

'Just think about those who have passed along the circle before us and love them for what they did as they passed by.'

'Of course,' he went on, 'It's not just the look of the place and the cutting of the stone that they have left for us. There is more than that to love them for.'

He now seemed to use the word 'love' instead of 'thank'.

'The past people have left us much besides. It's in the very walls,' and his hands felt down the pillars gently, scarcely touching the surface.

He then said, as we wandered down the nave, his hands never resting, 'It's like touching copper – I can feel a sensation when the hand is not quite on the metal.' I wondered about this and he could sense my doubt.

'You will agree,' he went on, 'that the power of thought can create or destroy; well here for eight hundred years there has been a continuous mist of prayer and song; they have left the mark of their strength and purpose as a patina on the stone. Just as brain waves register on a machine. And it makes this and other places like it blessed to the mind and healing to the touch.

'Of course, it works the other way too, if you don't guard your sacred places from the uncaring ways of casual wanderers, they will become as have our cathedrals, not places of prayer, but objects to gaze at and fill the minutes till the bus leaves. Remember the Caves at Lascaux where the walls became infected by the breath of countless people till the frescoes began to fade. Careless thoughts can corrupt as did the tourists' breath in those caves. This place is too important to risk.'

He ran his hands again down the side of a pillar and his eyes shone. I thought again for a moment of what he said about the 'healing touch' of the place.

'Ah,' he said, 'that must wait for another time – time – time.'

Then I felt a gentle dig in the ribs and my wife Esther's

voice saying, 'Time you stirred, he's finishing,' and a voice saying, 'And now to "God the Father, God the Son and God the Holy Spirit". Hymn two-hundred-and-five.'

Billy Wootton

Billy Wootton

DO YOU believe that places can bring sickness and misfortune to their owners and occupiers? Certainly we all know of houses with associated histories of bad luck. But in this case it was land itself, not a house, which seems to have carried a curse. See what you think.

I first heard the name Billy Wootton nearly forty years ago, just after the war. He had been an earlier tenant of the land across the A3 from our house. I had thought only occasionally of him since those days until the Department of Transport decided to change the siting of the A3 and demanded that we should sell them part of the land. This was for the seemingly pointless straightening of the road to make it, some say, even more dangerous than it was before. The negotiations required that the deeds of the land to be taken had to be prised out of the vaults of Lloyds Bank in Guildford. As I looked through the deeds, it all came back to me – William Wootton, sometime tenant of the Priorsfield Estate and his bizarre story.

I must say at once that Billy Wootton, because that is how he is remembered, departed from the scene many years before my arrival. Indeed, I only know of him from one person who told me all of this story apart from what I now know from the deeds.

In 1946, my wife Esther and I started farming together, armed with little knowledge and some very old machinery, much of it converted horse-drawn equipment which we used behind an antique International tractor. The combination of inexperience and mechanical make-do resulted in frequent breakdowns. The 1946 harvest was one that I shall never forget. It rained well into September by which time the stooks of corn became old friends from the repeated turning and moving they required to stop the corn sprouting.

It was before the era of the combine harvester and we still relied on that remarkable machine, the binder; a magical contrivance that after a succession of what seemed impossibly complicated mechanical functions gave, at the end of its clickings and bangings, a neatly tied sheaf of oats or barley. Or so it should have been; but during that harvest we had nothing but trouble. The age of the binder, well over fifty years, or my inexperience, may have been to blame but whatever the reason it called for the frequent help of Jimmy Locke, the travelling mechanic from the West Surrey Farmers. From him I learnt all I know about Billy Wootton.

I remember three things about Jimmy Locke; first he was a small man; second his overalls were so impregnated with oil and axle grease that he shone like a black beetle; and last his nose – it hung there like a big friendly door-knocker. During that long wet summer Jimmy would, with the slightest encouragement and sometimes without, tell me stories of the farming characters whom he had known during his long

career as a mechanic. Despite many gaps in the story of Billy Wootton there are a surprising number of facts, thanks to Jimmy Locke being a 'detail' chap. He went into every detail in detail. We used to call him, behind his back of course, 'I lie – it was a Thursday' – after his craving for accuracy and credibility over events which had occurred decades earlier. If you were in a hurry this meticulous regard for the minutiae could be trying. That summer it rained so much that it passed the time to chat to Jimmy as he mended the binder. I must admit that thanks to his careful recounting of events I still have a picture of what went on during those years before the First War in the fields opposite our house across the A3.

Jimmy Locke began telling me about Billy Wootton because he said that he and I were similar and not just because we farmed the same land. To be told you are like someone else is certain to stimulate interest and a sure invitation for enquiry as to what the other person is like.

'Well, you are both great breakers of machines,' and Jimmy went into one of his cheerful guffaws.

'Oh thank you,' I said, as at that time I was a bit sensitive about my ability to crack castings without touching them and to cause bearings to run hot just by looking.

'No, not really the same,' said Jimmy. 'Billy used to break machines intentionally. Hit them with frustration. Really lose his temper with them and then expect me to mend them.

'It wasn't just hitting things,' said Jimmy, 'he drove his horses and his machinery and himself so hard. For instance he would try and plough or cultivate when it was far too dry. Anyone else would have packed up or never started. Not Billy, he would just go on till something broke and then sit down completely exhausted gazing into the distance towards Hindhead, tears rolling down his cheeks. It was when I found him like that one day that he told me about his problems. I understood then why this grown man was so childlike.'

Billy Wootton, apparently, took over the tenancy of the thirty acres at Priorswood and tried to make a go of it. He came back from the Boer War, having answered the call for anyone who could handle horses for the artillery, with a great desire to work for himself. This land was all he could afford; the problems of making a living off a few acres of poor sandy soil were considerable. He survived by helping out on bigger neighbouring farms at busy times – and he was single.

'Then in about 1905,' explained Jimmy, 'that was when I started as a mechanic so I remember the date, it seems that a young lady came to stay at Priorswood House. She was the niece of Mr and Mrs Graham, Billy's landlords. I don't know how it happened but the young girl and Billy became friends. Probably she was lonely because the Grahams never had any children themselves. Anyway she didn't have far to go through the woods to see Billy, only a few years older than herself, busy on his little farm.

'The friendship between the niece of the Grahams and the handsome young tenant flourished unknown to everyone else. At least, so they thought – but that sort of carry-on is seldom a secret in the country.' Jimmy gave a knowing wink.

'Billy always thought it was one of the maids at the house, who was a bit sweet on him, that told on them.'

No one knows how far the affair had progressed but it seems that Billy Wootton proposed marriage and that they were planning to wed secretly. But when the liaison was betrayed to them, the Grahams rejected the whole idea.

'When it all came out, it was the way they laughed at Billy,' said Jimmy.

The break-up was achieved quite simply by the niece never being invited to stay again. Although Billy tried to reach her by letter these were intercepted.

There can be no doubt that they were very much in love and although the girl can be criticized for not sticking by him, Billy never blamed her. It was a time of strictly observed proprieties; appearances must be maintained and different classes not intermarry – what would the neighbours say? That customs should break such a bond of love was sad and the consequences came in full measure to Billy, who went to pieces in heartbroken frustration. Within a few years, he had ruined his farm, smashed his machinery and, as Jimmy expressed it, reduced himself to a 'sad mess'. In 1910, as the deeds of the land reveal, William Wootton surrenders his tenancy as 'his affairs are in the hands of the Masters of Lunacy'. Billy had gone mad.

That is not quite the end of it and now I come to the worrying bit. You will remember I asked the question – could land itself carry a curse of misfortune or illness? Further examination of the deeds showed that Billy Wootton's immediate predecessor as tenant – a Mr Walker – also went mad. What is more, Mrs Graham, the owner of Priorswood, and aunt of Billy's girl, developed delusions. Esther remembers going to a tea-party at the old house at which she solemnly announced her engagement to the Foreign Secretary, Mr Anthony Eden. She too became a legal lunatic.

So we have a trail of lunacy leading up to the present owners – ourselves. Our own sanity must be a matter of opinion but we do take comfort from the fact that if there is a curse of madness going with the land it has all run down to the bottom where the Ministry of Transport have built their new road. Certainly if you stand there on a busy day you may soon conclude that some of the drivers have gone mad. I hope it is them, anyway – I don't feel ready yet to go the way of Billy Wootton and the others.

The party

The party

IT WAS HOT on the top of my head. The sun was making the climb up the hill quite an effort. I was on my way to see my 'old warrior', as I called him, who lived on the crest of the escarpment, and I was regretting the previous night. Each week I used to go and spend an hour or two with him. At first, I had thought I was doing him a favour but soon I came to realize there was something about him that was quite special; I always came down filled with happiness – no, more than that – peace. It was a long time ago but I can still remember the headache, the long climb and sitting in the shade of the old man's verandah.

When I got to the bottom of his garden he was there to meet me. I think he had watched me as I plodded up the hill.

'You look rough,' he said quietly. 'Come and sit down and I'll get you a lemon drink.'

I didn't have to explain that I was not up to much in the way of conversation. I can still feel the strength of the old man's grip on my upper arm as he led me to my seat. We sat looking out over the sun-baked land with our heads in the shade: it was bliss. After a long silence he said, 'I'm going to tell you about a party I was at when I was about your age; I've never forgotten it and what happened after.' He paused and went on, 'I wish I could understand what it was really all about.'

'Will I understand it?' I asked.

'No,' he said slowly, 'But remember it – don't try and understand it – just remember it.' He topped up our lemon drinks and I waited.

He began, 'It was just an ordinary Guest Night party, when we all dressed up a bit, entertained what you would call the "local talent", which if I remember rightly wasn't very marvellous; all drank a bit too much and all woke up the following morning wondering why on earth we had bothered.'

He looked sideways at me and slipped in, 'Just like you today my boy.'

My headache was not quite gone but I was interested so I just answered wanly, 'Thank you – please go on.'

He straightened his old army tunic which, though frayed round the bottom edge, he always wore. He continued, 'I suppose it made a bit of a break in the seemingly unending boredom of garrison duty. None of us liked it much in the Middle East – too hot – too many flies and a lot of cussed awkward civilians who were either causing trouble among themselves or complaining about our troops. Not that we had a bad bunch of chaps but many of them were young and fed up with being so far from home. Oh and the bugs – can't forget the bugs. They used to crawl out of the wood of the mess benches and bite us behind the knees. However, back to the Guest Night party.

'As I say, it started just as an ordinary sort of "do", a few drinks at the bar, a few passes at the local ladies – bless them – and then into dinner. It was during dinner that suddenly we heard the adjutant call for quiet as the CO wished to speak to us. Instantly, silence spread down the tables. I can still see that stocky fair-haired figure rising. "Gentlemen, I have just heard from HQ that our regiment is posted home. I'm telling you this now because tomorrow you will hear it in the market place and I wanted you to be able to say your goodbyes to all our charming guests." And then followed a polite reference to the way the locals had befriended us. This was complete nonsense really; most of them hated our guts and the ladies present, with a few exceptions, were there for what they could get out of us. Anyway the secret, if it could be called such, was out and then, by Jove, that Guest Night turned into a real celebration.

'As you can imagine – the party became rather noisy. The conversation became a yelling match of jokes about what we were going to do when we got home and how we would never want to see sand again, even on a beach. I can remember too a few suggestions as to what we could do with those hideously uncomfortable issue helmets and I can tell you planting them out with geraniums was the only polite one I heard.'

The old man clearly enjoyed that memory but after a quiet chuckle he resettled himself and I could feel he was getting to the nub of his story. He was almost ignoring me now; he was reliving it all unselfconsciously, and was, I think, anxious to get on with it.

'Everything was in full swing,' he carried on, 'when I

suddenly became aware of the adjutant. He was standing in the tent entrance holding a writing tablet, the sort that all adjutants in all armies carry round to give themselves something to write notes on. Now I knew what he was up to because it was a habit he had. He would walk into the mess and just when you were letting your hair down a bit, he'd sneak up on you and you would find yourself next day on some futile desert trek or worse still taking a patrol through the Suk – ugh I hated that – smelly, hot and those wretched little boys – so embarrassing. I was determined not to get caught because I was rather enjoying myself so I adopted what we in the military world call a "low profile", which in this case consisted of turning my back and keeping my lady guest in intense conversation, hoping that by doing so I should escape notice or that the adjutant would think twice before interrupting.

'Of course, it didn't work. The adjutant was looking for me and me alone. I should explain that he and I, although not exactly on friendly terms, did have a sort of mutual respect. I suppose it stemmed from us both having soldiered together at various times. We had both been in the same lot in a rather unfortunate affair in northern France – not to mention the Huns. I was quite young but had been around a fair bit and if I was young the rest of the mess seemed just boys.

'No, the adjutant was not a man to pick on you out of spite and I suppose I ought to have felt pleased to be singled out. Frankly I wasn't. He tapped me on the shoulder. "No Adj," I said, "Not me, not the Suk again please."

' "No," he said slowly, "It's not the Suk, it's a special job."

He handed over the duty note and then took it back and turned it over.

' "Don't look at it tonight, don't spoil your evening; there's no hurry – early tomorrow morning will do." '

The old soldier moved the flap of his tunic and went on, 'I tucked away the note and tried to forget about it but, of course, the girl I was with wanted to know what it was all about. I got fed up with being pestered; anyway the adjutant was watching me, I felt sure; making certain that I was not spreading around my "special duty". After a few minutes I made some excuses. The party was over for me. I felt sick with anticipation. I walked back slowly through the lines. I leant against the tent pole, cold sober in the chill air, and pulled the note out. In the desert moonlight I could just read the orderly clerk's carefully written instructions.'

My old warrior was getting tired, I could see, but when I suggested that he paused in his story and rested awhile he waved it aside and said, 'No – I must go on. I must get it over. Well I walked back to the sergeant's mess and asked the orderly to tell my sergeant I wanted a word with him. He was a typical NCO, tough as leather with a bitten-back mouth like a clam and his hands were huge and hard; I remember his knuckles shone like marble when he grasped anything. No imagination – just obedience and yet these NCOs were the backbone of the army – "cement of the Empire" they were called.

' "Special job tomorrow, sergeant".

' "Sir," he barked back.

' "Bring your bag of things," I added.'

The old man paused in his story, then turned his broad shoulders round and took a small box from a shelf. He opened the box and handed me a writing tablet.

'Read that; no, on second thoughts I'll read it. I don't suppose you would understand the military abbreviations.'

He was standing now looking down at me with his eyes as blue as the Tuscan sky. I could see his thumb-nail sink into the wax as he read, 'Lucillus Sextus, Centurion, tomorrow Friday, you will proceed to the hill called Golgotha where you will crucify three Jews, two thieves and one they call the King of the Jews. Ensure all are dead and taken down by the ninth hour. Signed Pontius Pilatus. Governor of Judea.'